The Tree

by Giulia Verzariu
illustrated by Alex Wallner

Pre-Decodable 11

McGraw Hill Education

Bothell, WA • Chicago, IL • Columbus, OH • New York, NY

MHEonline.com

Send all inquiries to:
McGraw-Hill Education
8787 Orion Place
Columbus, OH 43240

ISBN: 978-0-02-140716-3
MHID: 0-02-140716-9

Printed in China

10 11 12 13 14 DSS 28 27 26 25 24

The  has .

tree branches

The  has 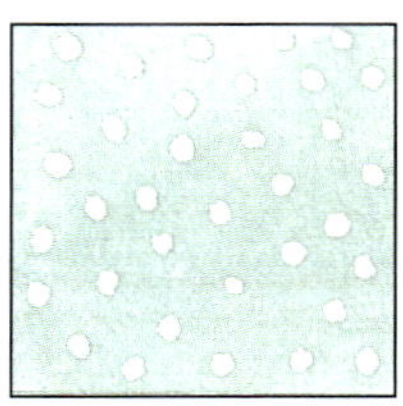.

tree snow

The  has  and .

tree birds flowers

The  has  and .

tree squirrels leaves

The  has  .

tree falling leaves

The  has 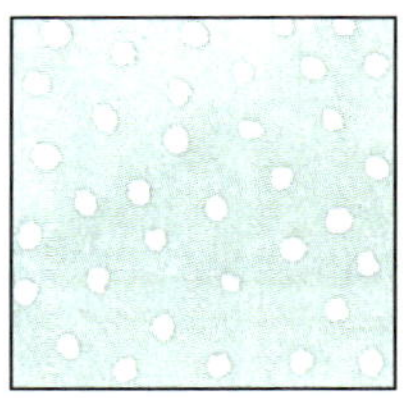.

tree

snow